CHILDREN OF DIVORCE

ParentsBook

ARNOLD L. STOLBERG / CHRISTOPHER W. CAMPLAIR
MICHAEL A. ZACHARIAS

AGS®
American Guidance Service
Circle Pines, Minnesota 55014-1796

ISBN: 0-88671-374-9

Contents

Introduction

As a parent, you are committed to building a strong, loving relationship with your child. As a parent who has gone through divorce, you are keenly aware of the painful changes your child is coping with as your family adjusts to new pressures and stresses. You know better than anyone how your child is doing in his or her adjustment to family change. Your willingness to have your child participate in the *Children of Divorce* program says a great deal about the depth of your care and concern. As the program begins, you'd probably like to know more about its goals, and about the role you can play in your child's experience.

Children of Divorce is a support program to help children adjust to divorce. In a comfortable, welcoming group setting, children meet to talk about feelings, share experiences, and learn new skills to help them cope with the changes in their lives. At home, children complete a workbook of activities that helps them practice new skills and explore personal concerns. Some of these activities are for parents and children to work on together as a way of strengthening their relationship and improving family communication. This "homework" is the primary way you can help and support your child during the program.

What Is the Program?
Studies have shown that divorce can, for a time, affect children's social and emotional development, as well as their school performance. The *Children of Divorce* program, led by a teacher, guidance counselor, or other trained professional, encourages children to talk about their feelings, learn how to solve problems and control their anger, and build their self-esteem. Many children whose parents are divorced feel frightened and alone.

Being in a group with other children from divorce can
help them see that they are not so different after all.

Each of the twelve sessions includes both skill-building
and self-esteem activities (Special Topics) and discussion. The sessions are:

Session 1: Welcome to the Group
Session 2: What are Feelings?
Session 3: Causes and Consequences of Feelings
Session 4: Telling Others How We Feel
Session 5: New Ways to Communicate
Session 6: Putting Our Feelings Into Words
Session 7: Self-Control and Problem Solving
Session 8: Step by Step by Step
Session 9: "That's Not My Problem!"
Session 10: "We're the Experts Now!"
Session 11: Learning About Anger
Session 12: Practicing Anger Control and Saying
             Goodbye to the Group

The Children's Newspaper. As part of each group session, children prepare items for a newspaper that they
plan, write, and publish together. The newspaper
serves as a record of their group that they can take with
them at the end of the program.

Program Materials. Materials for participants and
parents include the *KidsBook* and the *ParentsBook*.
During the first session, your child will receive a copy of
the *KidsBook*, which contains activities to do before
each session. The *KidsBook* contains three kinds of
activities. Many activities are for use in upcoming sessions. Some activities are for your child to do privately.
Some, called Parent-Child activities, are for you and
your child to do or to discuss together.

Most of the *KidsBook* activities give your child the
choice of writing or drawing. Cartoons that children
draw themselves are used to teach many of the skills.
These cartoons are explained later in the Introduction.

The *ParentsBook* is your key to the *Children of Divorce*
program. Here you'll find descriptions of each of the
Parent-Child activities in the *KidsBook*. Your main role
in these activities is to encourage your child and to discuss with her or him some of the issues raised in the
group sessions. Some activities ask that you help your
child practice some of the new skills. You will find sam-
ple questions and comments that can help guide your
conversations.

How You Can Be Involved
You'll find that the time you spend with your child on
the *Children of Divorce* activities can help you build a
stronger, more open relationship with your child. The
activities can help you and your child talk about sub-
jects and issues that you may have wanted to discuss,
but were uncertain how to begin.

Your involvement in the *Children of Divorce* program is
important. It has been shown that the program, which
has been developed and used with hundreds of children
and parents over the past eleven years, helps children
most when their parents are involved. Ideally, both
custodial and noncustodial parents will participate in
the program. This could mean working on the Parent-
Child exercises with your child by phone or even
through the mail.

The *KidsBook* activities group members are to do for
each session are a means for children to apply what
they've learned, reflect privately on their own feelings
and situation, and participate fully in the group. You

can help the most by showing your interest and encouraging your child to do the *KidsBook* activities.

If you find you are unable to do the Parent-Child exercises with your child, you can still help by encouraging and supporting your child's involvement in the program. If you cannot participate, you may wish to inform the group leader.

The Question of Confidentiality

Children need to talk about family matters, but be assured that your family's privacy will be respected throughout the *Children of Divorce* program. The confidentiality rule, explained at the first session, requires that any information shared in the group must not be discussed outside the group. If you are concerned about confidentiality, be sure to talk to your child's group leader.

Using the Parentsbook

Like the *KidsBook,* the *ParentsBook* is organized by session. Each session's purpose and objectives are explained. These activities may require writing or drawing a cartoon, cutting out pictures, practicing a skill, or discussing feelings or issues. Your role is either to do the activity with your child or, more frequently, to look over your child's work and talk about it together.

Setting Aside Time to Work Together. You can expect the ParentsBook activities to take about 30 to 60 minutes each week. To get in the habit of doing the activities, try getting together with your child each week at the same time. You might wish to schedule your time together a day or so after your child's group meeting, when memories of the discussion are fresh. Choose a quiet, comfortable place to do the activities together.

Be a Cheerleader! Your attitude toward the program
and the activities can be a great motivator for your
child. If you are enthusiastic about the program, it's
likely your child will be too. You can help by making a
commitment to work in the *ParentsBook* each week,
encouraging your child to do all the assigned *KidsBook*
activities, and reminding him or her to bring the
KidsBook to each session. You are asked at the end of
each chapter in the *Parentsbook* to make sure your child
has done all the *KidsBook* activities for the next session.
You need not read or examine your child's work, but do
show, by your attentiveness, the importance of doing the
activities.

Offering Help. If your child appears to be having difficulty with some of the *KidsBook* exercises, feel free to
offer your help. Whether or not your child accepts help,
your offer shows that you are interested and willing to
be involved.

Using the Cartoons. As explained earlier, the program
uses cartoons to help teach children how to cope with
strong feelings, solve problems, and control anger. Your
child's *KidsBook* contains copies of these cartoons that
you will be working on or discussing together.

The Talking and Feeling Cartoon shows step-by-step
how to identify and talk about feelings, link feelings
to events, and ask for help with strong feelings. The
Problem-Solving Cartoon shows how to solve problems
using an easy-to-follow system, the Problem-Solving
Steps. The Anger-Control Cartoon shows your child
how to remain calm when he or she is feeling angry.

Ask your child to show you the cartoons and explain
how they work. You'll probably think of many situations in which your child could use the cartoons to cope
with a strong feeling, solve a problem, or deal with

anger. You might want to suggest that he or she use the cartoons when such situations arise.

Helping Your Child Practice the Skills. Many of the Parent-Child exercises ask that you help your child practice the new skills he or she is learning in the group. You can do this by noticing times your child seems to need help with a problem or strong feeling and offering your assistance. For example, if your child is upset because you can't afford to buy her the coat she wants, suggest that you look at the Talking and Feeling Cartoon together. You can use the Problem-Solving Cartoon and the Anger- Control Cartoon in the same way for appropriate situations.

Talking With Your Child

Many of these activities encourage you to talk with your child about feelings connected with the divorce. Since many adults, as well as children, have difficulty talking about feelings, this can be challenging. Here are some guidelines you may find helpful:

Encouraging Your Child to Talk. Children often give cues, in words or behavior, that they are troubled. Parents know their children's cues better than anyone else. If your child seems sad or angry, you can help him or her talk about it by saying, "Gee, you've got a big frown. Are you feeling sad?" or "You seem pretty angry! Want to talk?" Asking your child for specific examples can help you focus on the issue together. For instance, if your child says, "I'm scared sometimes," you could ask about the last time she or he felt scared. Asking where your child was, who he or she was with, and what happened right before the feeling can help you understand more about your child's concerns.

Handling Difficult Situations. If, at some point in your discussions about the divorce, your child criticizes you or says something hurtful, try not to react defensively. Instead, listen to your child and acknowledge that you hear and understand by saying, "Yes, I've heard that kids from divorced families sometimes feel that way. I can understand that you feel . . ." Or, you might suggest that the two of you solve a specific problem together. If you like, ask for some time to think about the issue before you discuss it with your child. It may be helpful to talk with a friend first.

You don't necessarily need to explain or provide a solution to difficult problems. You can often help best by simply supporting your child's efforts to discuss feelings with you.

Sometimes children go "too far." You know your boundaries. If you feel your child is being disrespectful or deliberately hurtful, it's appropriate to say, "It is not okay for you to put me down," or "I feel angry when you talk to me like that," and postpone the discussion.

If your child expresses attitudes or ideas or you find offensive or out of step with your family values, try to respond calmly but directly:

"I'm not comfortable with your solution to this problem. We don't lie in this family."
"I understand that you don't like the person I'm dating. But it's up to me to choose my friends."
"Please don't use that kind of language. It makes me angry and then I can't talk with you the way I want to."

Being the Parent. Sometimes as a result of divorce, children may sense a parent's distress and try to give support; in effect, the child takes on the role of the parent. This is an unhealthy situation for both parents and children. You can certainly encourage discussion by sharing some of your own feelings and experiences with your child, such as, "I'm lonely too."

However, it is important that children feel that they can depend on their parents for their emotional needs. Assure your child, "I'm your mom (dad), and I'm here to give *you* support."

Respecting Your Child's Privacy. As you know, when children get older, they want to make some of their own decisions.   One way they express their independence is by choosing how and when to share their private thoughts. Show your child you are willing to talk, but try not to force a discussion. (It won't work anyway.) Make an effort to be available to talk when your child appears to be ready.

It's also important that your child feels his or her privacy is respected. Some children find it difficult to express their private thoughts and feelings. Early in the program in particular, children may be reluctant or embarrassed to share personal information. If children sense parents are prying, they may "shut down" communication entirely. Try to respect your child's wishes if she or he does not want to discuss group meetings or activities from time to time. Also, when you check to see that the *KidsBook* activities have been done, let your child know that "on-your-own" activities are for his or her eyes alone.

When You Have Questions. . .

If you have questions about the program or your child's progress in the group, don't hesitate to call your child's group leader. You might also wish to consult the leader if you feel you need help in communicating with your child.

References for Further Reading

1. An excellent guide for talking with your child is
   Haim De Ginott's *Between Parent and Child* (New
   York: Avon, 1969).

2. *Strengthening Stepfamilies* by Elizabeth Einstein
   and Linda Albert (Circle Pines, MN: American Guidance Service, 1986) and *STEP/Parent's Handbook*
   by Don Dinkmeyer and Gary D. McKay (Circle
   Pines, MN: American Guidance Service, 1989) can
   provide helpful information on a variety of parenting
   topics.

Learning About Feelings

Children of divorce are often aware of their parents' anger, depression, and anxiety. They may mirror these emotions and react to their feelings without understanding them or knowing their basis. Eric may not realize that the reason he's angry is that his father forgot his birthday. He may show his anger in ways that alienate and infuriate his friends, parents, and teachers. Instead of getting the support and understanding he needs, Eric only makes his problems worse.

It has been shown that when children understand the connections between their feelings, their behavior, and the events in their lives, they are more likely to have successful relationships with others.

In the next group session, your child will be considering what feelings are, how to tell one feeling from another, how to find out what our feelings are telling us. Your child also will see that many of her* feelings about divorce are shared by others in the group, a fact many children find comforting.

This week's KidsBook activities will prepare children for the next session by:

- introducing the topic of feelings in a fun, positive way
- encouraging them to identify their feelings and be aware of when they have feelings
- helping them realize they are not the only ones whose parents are divorced

How you can help

The following KidsBook activities are for you and your child to do together. Here are suggestions for ways you can be involved.

KidsBook Activity 1-2

With my parents' help, cut out ten to twenty pictures from magazines and newspapers that show people having strong feelings. Bring them to the next group meeting.

At their next session, children will use these pictures to make a "feelings" collage. This activity increases your child's awareness of feelings and of the ways people's faces and bodies show what they are feeling.

Help your child collect magazines and newspapers and encourage her to select pictures that show a variety of feelings.

You might say:

---

* The use of masculine and feminine pronouns in reference to children is varied throughout the ParentsBook. The information presented, however, applies to children of either sex.

2

"Where did we see that photograph of the family who lost their home in a fire? Those faces showed strong feelings."

"What feelings do you see in this picture?"

"Can you find a copy of *Sports Illustrated?* It usually has lots of feelings pictures."

"Let's see if we can find pictures of people feeling happy."

As you work on the activity together, you may wish to talk about ways the members of your family show their feelings.

KidsBook Activity 1-3
Make a list of everyone I can think of whose parents are divorced or separated. Discuss my list with my mom and dad.

This activity helps children see that divorce is part of many people's lives, that they are not the only ones whose parents are divorced. The list is for you and your child to discuss. It won't be shared with the group.

Discuss your child's list with her and suggest additions that occur to you. You might say:

"We seem to know a lot of people who are divorced or whose parents are divorced. Are you surprised we know so many?"

"You can't think of anyone but you? What about your cousin Don? His parents are divorced."

"Are any of the kids in your class living with just their mom or dad? What about the kids in the group? They all come from divorced families, right?"

"How does it feel to know so many people have divorce in their families?"

Summing Up

After you've helped your child with these activities and checked to see that the others have been done, sum up the experience and be encouraging. For example:

"Are you finding out some new things about feelings?"

"You really did a great job in your KidsBook!"

"It's fun doing this together."

"I think doing these activities together will help us get along better. I'm here to help if you need me."

Where Do Feelings Come From?

In the next group session, your child will practice identifying feelings, see that events in life can bring on feelings, and consider the effects our feelings have on the people around us. Your child will also see that people with feelings in common can begin to trust each other.

This week's KidsBook activities will prepare children for the next session by:

- helping them understand where feelings come from and how their bodies are affected when they have strong feelings
- encouraging them to talk with parents about feelings
- helping them feel comfortable sharing feelings with others

How you can help

The following KidsBook activities are for you and your child to do together. Here are suggestions for ways you can be involved.

KidsBook Activity 2-1

Show in pictures or words a time I had strong feelings. Then talk with my parents about what feelings are and where they come from.

This activity is for you and your child to discuss. It won't be shared with the group.

During the week, try to talk with your child about feelings. If your child is reluctant at first, let him know you are interested and available.

You might begin such a talk when you notice your child expressing a strong feeling, such as anger or joy. Make note of what brought on the feeling or ask about it. You could recall other times your child has had a strong emotional response to something that happened (such as getting angry when someone teased him, being happy when he got a good grade on a test). You could also mention a time you yourself had strong feelings.

You might say:

"I remember how I felt inside the night the dog ran away. My heart was pounding and my stomach hurt. How did *you* feel when . . ."

Look at your child's work. Tell him how you felt when you read the story or looked at the picture. Then ask your child to think about how he showed his feelings. You might say:

"I see you were angry when I told you to turn off the TV
and get ready for bed. I was angry too. What exactly
was happening at the time? What were you watching?
How did you feel when I told you to stop watching TV?
What happened to your body? What were you thinking?"

"I know some of these feelings are tough to talk about.
Let's try thinking about a happy time first. Can you
remember when you felt especially happy? What happened? How did your body feel?"

KidsBook Activity 2-2

*List times during the week when I felt angry, sad, happy,
or worried. Describe where I was, what happened to
bring on the feeling, and how my body felt. Then talk
with my parents about my list.*

In the group, your child will discuss these experiences
and see how events can bring about feelings.

Look over the list your child completed. Discuss one or
two of the feelings your child described in terms of how
his body felt and how he looked to others when he had
the feeling. You could say:

"When you were feeling worried, how did your face feel?
Did your jaw feel tense? How did your stomach feel?
How do you think you looked to other people?"

If you can, tell your child what you saw him do or heard
him say at the time. You might also mention a time
when you had a similar feeling. Tell him how your body
was affected and how you think you looked to others.

Then talk with your child about how he feels right now.
You could ask:

"How does your stomach feel now, while we're talking about these things? Do you feel tense or tight? Why do you think you feel that way?"

KidsBook Activity 2-4

Circle words on a list that describe my feelings.

This activity is for you and your child to discuss. It won't be shared with the group.

Do the same activity your child has done. On your own, circle the words listed below that describe how you think your child has been feeling the past week:

excited	loved	sad
shy	happy	impatient
silly	peaceful	worried
jealous	moody	smart
cared about	depressed	glad
satisfied	lonely	confused
calm	tired	special
guilty	lucky	talkative
afraid	cheerful	angry
discouraged	lazy	generous
encouraged	pleased	surprised
hopeful	disappointed	hopeless
bored	helpless	scared

Then look at each other's lists and compare them. Talk about times you've noticed your child having various feelings. You might say:

"We checked a lot of the same feelings. Are you surprised? Do you sometimes think no one notices when you're feeling something?"

"Can you tell me what you felt confused about? I'd like to know. Your feelings are very important to me."

"Were you afraid when I got home later than I said I would? I'm so sorry that happened."

Summing Up

After you've helped your child with these activities and checked to see that the other has been done, sum up the experience and be encouraging. For example:

"It helps me to know which feelings you're comfortable talking about and which ones you like to keep private."

"Do you think you would feel okay talking with me more about the divorce? What could I do to make it easier?"

"Feelings can be hard to talk about, but I think we both learned a lot. How did you feel about the activities?"

"I'm impressed by the good work you're doing. You seem to be learning a lot in your group."

How Our Feelings Affect Our Actions

In the next group session, your child will continue to discuss the "ripple effect" of feelings: from event, to feeling, to behavior, to the reactions of other people. Your child will also explore various ways to communicate feelings and will work on building trusting relationships with group members.

This week's KidsBook activities will prepare children for the next session by:

- making them aware of how events can trigger feelings and reactions to feelings
- encouraging them to talk and write about their feelings with parents' help

How you can help

The following KidsBook activity is for you and your child to do together. Here are suggestions for ways you can be involved.

KidsBook Activity 3-2

Share with my parents my Talking and Feeling Cartoons and the things I've learned about feelings.

The Talking and Feeling Cartoon is a writing and drawing exercise that helps your child better understand the causes and effects of feelings. When your child shows you her work, let her know you're interested. If she is reluctant to talk, you might say:

"I see your KidsBook activities are about feelings again this week. Shall we get a snack and look over the activities together?"

"Would you like to talk about your KidsBook activities now? I'd like to see what you're working on this week."

Look over your child's descriptions of her feelings, what caused them, how she reacted to them physically, and how other people reacted to them. Praise her efforts, even if she left a line or two blank. If you like, encourage your child to complete the activity, and then talk about it. You might say:

"Tell me more about what happened to make you jealous. Maybe I can help see that it doesn't happen again."

"I see that you felt hungry when you were excited. I'm usually too excited to eat!"

"I could tell you felt angry when you lost the game. Can you remember how your body felt inside? Do you remember what you did? I do!"

"Why do you think Grandpa told you to stop complaining? Did he understand why you felt lonely?"

Compare your child's descriptions with what she wrote or drew on the Talking and Feeling Cartoons. You might say:

"This is good! Those people *do* look surprised at what you said."

If your child had trouble thinking of times she had strong feelings, help by talking about times you noticed. You might say:

"You can remember a time you felt angry but not a time you felt happy? How about when you went fishing with Dad? Were you happy then?"

Summing Up

After you've helped your child with this activity and checked to see that the other has been done, sum up the experience and be encouraging. For example:

"How can you tell when other people are having feelings? How do you think I can tell when you're having a happy feeling or a sad feeling?"

"Some feelings are hard to think about, aren't they? You did a great job on this activity."

"These Talking and Feeling Cartoons are good at helping you figure things out, aren't they?"

"Do you want to talk more about the work you're doing in the group? I'm here if you need me."

Talking About Feelings

Children need to find constructive ways to express strong feelings. In the next session, your child will learn ways to control his reactions to strong feelings ("cool-downs"), as well as cues ("Let's Talk Cues") that will let others know when he needs emotional support.

This week's KidsBook activities will prepare children for the next session by:

- showing that divorce is a stressful event that can cause certain problems and reactions
- increasing their understanding of the connection between events, feelings, and behavior
- helping them see the causes and effects of feelings

How you can help

The following KidsBook activity is for you and your child to do together. Here are suggestions for ways you can be involved.

KidsBook Activity 4-2

Do a Talking and Feeling Cartoon 2 for each of the two problems I chose and write out the Message for each. Share the cartoons with my parents and talk about the problems.

During the session, your child will use these cartoons to work on constructive ways of dealing with strong feelings. The cartoons require your child to figure out the Message, which relates feelings to specific events.

Look over your child's cartoons. Help him fill in any panels he has left blank. Comment on how useful the cartoons are in helping you understand his feelings and concerns about the divorce. Discuss the Message. If he has trouble discovering the Message, offer your help and encouragement. You might say:

"You did a great job in this cartoon showing what happened first, how you felt, and how others reacted. Now let's work on the Message together."

"You worked hard on this one. I can see you understand how problems and feelings can be connected. What word would name the feeling you had?"

"Sometimes it's hard to figure out the Message, especially if a lot is going on in your life. Let's go through this cartoon step-by-step and see if we can figure out together what caused the problem."

Summing Up

After you've helped your child with this activity and checked to see that the other has been done, sum up the experience and be encouraging. For example:

"How do you feel about talking these things over together? I think it brings us closer."

"Sometimes it's hard to figure out exactly how we feel about what's happening in our family because we're part of it. I think you did a good job sorting things out."

"I can see there are things I can do to make life happier around here."

"You're doing a great job in this KidsBook. I think it's helping both of us."

PARENTSBOOK 5

"Let's Talk" Cues

In the next group session, your child will practice skills for communicating feelings and will learn ways to get support from others for the changes she is making.

This week's KidsBook activities will prepare children for the next session by:

- strengthening their understanding of the relationship between events, feelings, and behavior
- giving them practice using their cool-downs and Let's Talk Cue to let parents know they need to talk about their strong feelings

How you can help

The following KidsBook activity is for you and your child to do together. Here are suggestions for ways you can be involved.

*Do two Talking and Feeling Cartoons 3. Show my car-
toons to my parents and tell them my cool-down and
Let's Talk Cue.*

This activity is for you and your child to discuss. It
won't be shared with the group.

Your child will be drawing two Talking and Feeling Cartoons that show the cool-down and Let's Talk Cue she
has chosen. The cool-down helps your child calm down
before reacting to a situation. The Let's Talk Cue is her
special signal to you that she has strong feelings and
wants to talk. Both are intended to help your child
express feelings in clear, positive ways that will invite
support from others.

Go over the cartoons with your child and talk about the
Let's Talk Cue. The cue might be physical (a hand signal, body posture, foot tapping), verbal (a code or a
direct request), or written. Use the problems your child
showed in the cartoons to talk about how, when, and in
what situations she might use the Let's Talk Cue.
Assure your child that you will look out for her cue and
respond as best you can. You might say:

"That's a great cue. If I saw you use it, I'd know right
away you wanted to talk. Let's pretend you used it to let
me know about this problem. How would you like me to
help?"

"So your cue will be wearing your purple tee shirt. I'll be
on the lookout for it!"

During the week, when you notice your child using her
cue, try to respond immediately. Let her know that you
saw the cue and want to understand what she is feeling.
Listen and offer support. If your child has a positive

first experience using the cue, she will be more likely to use it again.

You might say:

"I just noticed your cue. Let's sit down now and talk about what's bothering you. I'm glad you let me know you needed to talk."

"There's the cue! Let me put the groceries away—then we'll sit down and talk."

Summing Up

After you've helped your child with this activity and checked to see that the others have been done, sum up the experience and be encouraging. For example:

"Your Let's Talk Cue is a good way to let me know you need some time to talk."

"I see from your cartoons that you understand how certain things that happen can make us feel angry, or sad, or lonely. You're really catching on fast. I'm proud of you."

Putting Feelings Into Words

When children must make hard choices, they need the self-control to choose what should be done, instead of what they'd rather do. Learning a step-by-step approach to problem solving helps them think before they act.

In the next group session, your child will learn how to use Problem-Solving Steps to help make good decisions when faced with situations requiring self-control. Your child will also see how divorce-related situations can affect feelings.

This week's KidsBook activities will prepare children for the next session by:

- helping them assess and improve their skills in communicating feelings
- encouraging them to communicate openly with their parents

How you can help

The following KidsBook activities are for you and your
child to do together. Here are suggestions for ways you
can be involved.

KidsBook Activity 6-1

*Show a friend and me having a conversation. Talk about
it with my mom and dad.*

This activity is for you and your child to discuss. It
won't be shared with the group.

Look over your child's dialogue and the rating scale he
filled out. (The scale has children consider how they feel
with friends and how well they communicate what they
feel.) You might say:

"Did you want your friend to answer you the way he
did? Could he have helped you more by saying something else?"

"Were you glad you talked to your friend about your feelings? Will you do it again?"

"You feel *okay* when you're with friends. What would
help you feel better?"

"It's great that you almost always tell your friends how
you feel. That's what friends are for."

You may disagree with your child's rating. For instance,
if your child thinks he's a poor communicator and you
rate him good, ask him why he feels that way. Or, if
your child thinks he's a good communicator, and you feel
he's secretive, you could say, "I think you have some
work to do," and offer some examples. Your objective
reactions can be helpful.

KidsBook Activity 6-2

Finish sentences about my feelings and talk about these feelings with my mom and dad.

This activity is for you and your child to discuss. It won't be shared with the group.

Read the sentences your child completed. Try to comment on both the feelings he continues to have and those that have changed. You might say:

"I didn't know you've been feeling worried lately. That's a change for you, isn't it? Can you tell me why you're feeling that way now?"

"Is it easier for you to talk about feelings now than it used to be? Is it easier to talk to me about your feelings? What can I do to help?"

"I've noticed lately that it seems easier for you to talk about feelings. Do you think that's true?"

"Which feelings are hardest to talk about? Why? How can I help make it easier?"

Summing Up

After you've helped your child with these activities, sum up the experience and be encouraging. For example:

"I'm getting a real sense of how you're feeling these days. Thanks for helping me understand you."

"You seem to be getting along a lot better with your friends lately. I know it was hard right after the divorce."

"You don't seem to think you're very good at letting people know how you feel. But I think you're getting a lot better at it."

PARENTSBOOK 7

Problem-Solving Steps

In the next group session, your child will practice using Problem-Solving Steps in various situations and will discuss feelings or problems that are troubling her.

This week's KidsBook activities will prepare children for the next session by:

- helping them learn to use Problem-Solving Steps
- encouraging them to express feelings constructively and appropriately

How you can help

The following KidsBook activities are for you and your child to do together. Here are suggestions for ways you can be involved.

KidsBook Activity 7-1

Match the Problem-Solving Steps with the pictures that fit them. Then discuss the steps with my parents.

This activity is for you and your child to discuss. It won't be shared with the group.

Ask your child to explain the five Problem-Solving Steps. Suggest you try out the steps together. You might say:

"Let's try using these steps. Remember the time you wanted to go swimming with your friends and I wanted you to babysit your brother so I could go grocery shopping? What were your choices?"

Use the steps with several problems.

KidsBook Activity 7-2

Describe the problems shown in three pictures and show similar problems I've been having. Use Problem-Solving Steps to solve the problems, and discuss with my parents.

In the group, your child will use these problems to practice the Problem-Solving Steps.

Look over the problems your child described as similar to the problems pictured. Review the Problem-Solving Steps and discuss how you could apply them to each problem. You might say:

"I didn't realize you weren't understanding your math homework. Let's see how the Problem-Solving Steps can help. What choices do you have to solve this problem? What might happen if you asked your teacher for extra help? What's the best choice for you? What do you think will happen if you do that?"

KidsBook Activity 7-3

Write a letter telling how I feel about my family to share with my parents.

Your child has been encouraged to share her letter with you. Spend some time talking about it. You could:

- read the letter and thank your child for being willing to share her feelings
- ask your child for a little time to think before you discuss this important letter

As you consider how to respond, keep in mind that even if you find elements of the letter disturbing, it's important to let your child know that you are always willing to talk. Help your child understand that having strong feelings is normal and talking about them is one way of dealing with them.

If you and your child find this activity to be a successful way to bring up and discuss important issues, you may wish to suggest using it other times.

Summing Up

After you've helped your child with these activities, sum up the experience and be encouraging. For example:

"Your letter about feelings was painful to read, but I think it will help us talk more honestly."

"Let me know if you use the Problem-Solving Steps to solve the problem you talk about in your letter. I'll bet the steps will help you sort things out."

Talking About Problems and Feelings

Children from divorced families sometimes feel responsible for events beyond their control. They need reassurance that some problems can't be solved by anyone, and others can be solved only by adults. In the next group session, your child will learn the difference between solvable and unsolvable problems and how to tell who is responsible for solving a problem. Your child also will have a chance to discuss his individual concerns related to divorce.

This week's KidsBook activities will prepare children for the next session by:

- helping them practice and apply their problem-solving skills
- helping them identify a major concern related to their parents' divorce

- providing opportunities to discuss with parents and their families their feelings about divorce

How you can help

The following KidsBook activities are for you and your child to do together. Here are suggestions for ways you can be involved.

KidsBook Activity 8-2

Solve two problems using the Problem-Solving Cartoon. Then talk over my work with my mom and dad.

This activity is for you and your child to discuss. It won't be shared with the group.

Look over your child's cartoons and ask him to explain each step. Since problem solving is difficult for children, you could offer suggestions as you go through each problem together. You might say:

"I see you chose to cancel your visit with Grandma so you could go to a birthday party. Can you think of any other ways you might solve that problem?"

"This is a hard problem for me too! You have two choices listed. I can think of another one."

"Solving problems is hard, isn't it? I always think of more choices when I talk to a friend about a problem. Does that happen to you too?"

KidsBook Activity 8-3

Finish sentences describing how I feel about my parents and talk about them with my mom and dad.

This activity is for you and your child to discuss. It won't be shared with the group.

The sentences your child has completed focus on his thoughts and feelings about his parents. This exercise can lead to a satisfying discussion between you and your child about some sensitive issues. However, you'll need to listen to and accept your child's impressions without becoming defensive or upset.

To guide the discussion, you might say:

"Would you mind if I spend a few minutes looking over what you've written? Then let's sit down and talk. I'm glad to know what you're thinking and feeling."

"I'm glad we're talking about these things. If it weren't for your KidsBook activities, I might not have known you felt this way. Which sentence was hardest for you to write?"

Summing Up

After you've helped your child with these activities and checked to see that the other has been done, sum up the experience and be encouraging. For example:

"These activities gave me a lot to think about. How did you feel about them?"

"That Problem-Solving Cartoon is useful, isn't it? I'd like us to try it the next time we have a disagreement, okay?"

"Thanks for sharing your feelings with me. I know it's not easy to do."

PARENTSBOOK 9

More on Problem Solving

Children need lots of practice solving problems. In the next group session, your child, along with other group members, will put on a pretend television talk show, "The WKID Show," during which they'll play divorce experts. They will also discuss their progress as problem solvers.

This week's KidsBook activities will prepare children for the next session by:

- giving them more practice in problem solving
- reviewing what is meant by solvable and unsolvable problems and by problem ownership
- having them rate themselves as problem solvers

How you can help

The following KidsBook activities are for you and your child to do together. Here are suggestions for ways you can be involved.

KidsBook Activity 9-1
Solve two more problems using the Problem-Solving Cartoon and talk with my mom and dad about my solutions.

This activity is for you and your child to discuss. It won't be shared with the group.

Look over these cartoons, in which your child has tried to solve problems about divorce. For each cartoon, decide together:

Is the solution fair? (Will it hurt your child or other people?)
Does it work? (Can your child do it?)
Is it easy to do, or hard to do?
What could happen if your child did it?

You might ask:

"Does this solution seem fair to you? Do you think it would seem fair to others?"

"If we picked this solution, no one would be happy. Can you think of some other possibilities? Sometimes it's hard to find one good solution, isn't it?"

To help guide your discussion, remember to:

- give reasons for your opinions
- focus on judging only the solution
- make clear that sometimes it's difficult to decide which solution is best
- emphasize that sometimes we pick solutions that don't work, but we can always try again

KidsBook Activity 9-2
With my parents, use the Problem-Solving Computer to decide what to do about three problems.

This activity is for you and your child to discuss. It won't be shared with the group.

The Problem-Solving Computer was introduced in the last group session. It points out what your child can do about a problem that she can and should solve, such as deciding whether to study for a test or play basketball. The computer also suggests what your child can do when she is faced with an unsolvable problem or one that isn't hers to solve.

Your child has been asked to show you the Problem-Solving Computer and explain how it works. Afterward, as you discuss the problems, you might ask:

"How would you use the Talking and Feeling Cartoon if a problem is not yours to solve?"

Summing Up

After you've helped your child with these activities and checked to see that the others have been done, sum up the experience and be encouraging. For example:

"These activities were challenging! You did a great job."

"Do you think you understand why you need to decide who owns a problem? Sometimes kids think they need to solve their parents' problems. Do you ever feel that way?"

"If you ever want help solving a problem, please ask me. I'd like to help."

PARENTSBOOK 10

Looking at Changes

Anger is one of the most common and powerful emotions felt by children from divorced families. In the next session, your child will consider anger: what causes us to feel angry, how we express our anger, and how to control our anger using a "cooling-down" strategy. Group members also will think about their experience in the group so far.

This week's KidsBook activities will prepare children for the next session by:

- helping them evaluate their skills in solving problems, understanding and expressing feelings, and being a friend
- helping them compare their old and new ways of dealing with anger
- encouraging them to talk about the changes they are making

How you can help

The following KidsBook activities are for you and your child to do together. Here are suggestions for ways you can be involved.

KidsBook Activity 10-1
With my parents, rate how well I'm doing in things like problem solving, listening, and talking about feelings.

This activity is for you and your child to discuss. It won't be shared with the group.

Help your child fill out the rating scale in KidsBook Activity 10-1. For each category, discuss how you would rate your child and how your child would rate himself. Talk about the ways you agree and disagree. You might say:

"Do you think you're just *okay* as a listener? I'd say you were *pretty good*. I've noticed quite an improvement."

"So you think you *need help* being a friend. Let's talk about that. Why do you feel that way?"

"Yes, I agree you're a *great* problem solver!"

If you can, offer examples of the improvements you've noticed and encourage efforts to change. For example:

"Last week when your sister borrowed your favorite pair of jeans without asking, I noticed that you talked to her about it instead of yelling at her and running to me. I was impressed! You're doing a good job using what you've learned in your group."

KidsBook Activity 10-2

Draw cartoons to show my old ways and new ways of dealing with anger. Talk about them with my mom and dad.

This activity is for you and your child to discuss. It won't be shared with the group.

Look over the cartoons your child drew in the KidsBook. Discuss the changes he has noticed in the way he deals with anger, and those you have noticed. If your child has left some frames blank, you might offer your help. If appropriate, suggest other ways your child might deal with anger.

Then discuss with your child the progress you've noticed him making, as well as the areas still needing improvement. You may wish to make a list together. Feel free to comment on areas other than anger control. For example:

Marcus is improving in:

- getting along with his sister
- doing his homework before he watches TV
- doing chores when he's asked

Marcus still has difficulty:

- telling Mom and Dad when he's lonely or depressed
- spending holidays with Dad and his new family
- controlling his angry outbursts

Be sure to tell your child how pleased you are at the progress he is making. Together, discuss ways you can help him improve.

Summing Up

After you've helped your child with these activities and checked to see that the other has been done, sum up the experience and be encouraging. For example:

"I didn't realize all the ways you've been changing. Did you?"

"It's hard to make changes. I'm proud of you for trying so hard."

"I know it feels uncomfortable sometimes, but it's important to try these new skills. You know you can always ask me for help."

PARENTSBOOK 11
All About Anger

Controlling anger takes practice. In the last Children of Divorce session, which is partly devoted to saying good-bye to the group, your child will be practicing anger-control skills.

This week's KidsBook activities will prepare children for the next session by:

- helping them choose their own way of controlling anger
- showing that parents can help them with their anger

How you can help

The following KidsBook activities are for you and your child to do together. Here are suggestions for ways you can be involved.

KidsBook Activity 11-1

With my mom and dad, choose my way of controlling my anger better at home.

During the session, your child will use her Anger Cool-Down in a role-play activity.

Begin by talking with your child about anger. Explain that everyone feels angry at times and that everyone has difficulty sometimes controlling anger. Talk about the advantages of controlling anger: it allows us to use our energy in more fun and productive ways, it preserves our relationships, it helps us solve problems instead of creating them. You may wish to give some examples of times you've been angry, how you reacted, and what happened.

Together, look over the cooling-down strategies listed in the KidsBook and try to think of others. As you consider them, ask yourself:

Which strategy would work best in your home?
Which strategy would fit best with your child's personality?
What does your child think will work?
Which strategy will allow you to help the most?

Help your child pick a strategy and discuss how she'll use it during the week. You might say:

"I think that's a good strategy for you. Now when I see you bouncing a basketball against the garage I'll know you're angry. Would you like me to ask you about it or leave you alone?"

KidsBook Activity 11-2

Make an Anger-Control Contract with my parents.

This activity is for you and your child to discuss. It won't be shared with the group.

The Anger-Control Contract on the next page is similar to the one in the KidsBook. Ask your child how you can help her honor her contract. Talk about some reward you could offer for using her Anger Cool-Down, such as going out for pizza or doing a fun activity together. Your support combined with a reward can be a good incentive.

Fill in your contract and sign both. Have your child do the same. Hang the contracts next to each other in a visible place, such as on the refrigerator or on your child's bedroom door.

Summing Up

After you've helped your child with these activities, sum up the experience and be encouraging. For example:

"It's normal to feel angry, but sometimes anger can cause us problems. How do you think your contract can keep us from arguing so much?"

"I feel good about our Anger-Control Contracts. How do you think they'll work for us?"

"Anger can feel scary because it's such a strong emotion. It helps me to talk about it. How about you?"

IMPORTANT NOTICE!

PLEASE POST IN A PROMINENT PLACE

ANGER-CONTROL CONTRACT

Name: ___________________________ Date: _______________

I will help _______________ control anger by:

____

____

and ____

_______________ can ask me for help anytime.

I agree to the terms of this contract for the week of _______

____
Your Signature

____
Your Child's Signature

Wrapping Up

Although the Children of Divorce group sessions have ended, you and your child are asked to do one more set of activities. These activities reinforce some important skills that your child will use now and in the future. As you work together, encourage your child to practice and use what he has learned in the group.

KidsBook Activity 12-2
Check with my parents on how well our Anger-Control Contracts are working.

Talk with your child about the Anger-Control Contracts. You might ask:

"How do you think our contracts are working? I feel good about them."

"Are you satisfied with your Anger Cool-Down? Does it seem to work, or do you want to try a different one?"

"How could we make the contracts work better?"

If your child has been controlling anger well, you may wish to reward him as you discussed last time. Show that you recognize and appreciate the good work your child is doing.

KidsBook Activity 12-3
Finish sentences on how I'm feeling about myself and my life. Discuss the sentences with my parents.

Look over your child's sentences, which may give you some insights into his self-esteem, his feelings about the future, and his feelings about your relationship. You might ask:

"It looks like things have gotten better for you since you joined the group. Now that the group is over, what can we do to help keep things that way?"

"You didn't finish the sentence *Something I like about myself is* . . . Let's talk about things *I* like about you. Maybe you'll get some ideas."

Writing a letter to your child

For a last activity, write a letter to your child. Tell him how he has grown and changed since he joined the Children of Divorce group. Mention the changes you have noticed in the way he expresses his feelings, deals with anger, solves problems. Compliment him on any improvements in his relationships with friends and family, his school performance, his attitudes or behavior. If you'd like, use the form that follows to get started.

Share the letter with your child. Be open to your child's opinions and impressions.

You may wish to plan a special activity together as a reward for your hard work over the past weeks. Congratulations on completing this program with your child!

Date: ___________

Dear _____________,

I'd like to tell you how I think you've grown over the past weeks. ___________________________________

____

____

____

____

____

____

____

____

____

____

____

____

____

____

Love,

____